This Book Belongs to:

Rebecca Chloe Simpson

It was given to me By:

Sarah Dueck (CLCC Kid's Pastor)

on:

22 September 2019.

3-MINUTE
DEVOTIONS

for
Little Hearts

Jean Fischer
Illustrated by David Miles

BARBOUR BOOKS
An Imprint of Barbour Publishing, Inc.

Print ISBN 978-1-68322-221-7

Cover and interior illustration: David Miles Illustration, www.davidmiles.us

Published by Barbour Books, an imprint of Barbour Publishing, Inc., P.O. Box 719, Uhrichsville, Ohio 44683, www.barbourbooks.com

Our mission is to publish and distribute inspirational products offering exceptional value and biblical encouragement to the masses.

Member of the
Evangelical Christian
Publishers Association

Printed in China.
05697   0617   DS

For all GOD's ChilDren,
young and olD

INTRODUCTION

My Special Time with God

There is a special time for everything.
There is a time for everything that
happens under heaven.
ECCLESIASTES 3:1

♥ ♥ ♥

God created day and night. Then He filled them up with all kinds of wonderful things for you to do. There is time for play and time for work. Time to learn and explore new things. Time for breakfast, lunch, and dinner. Time to rest. Time to sleep. So much time! But how much time do you have for God? The little lessons in this book will help you to spend at least three minutes a day with God. And as you learn to know Him better, you will want to spend more time with Him. You will want to be with Him all day and all night. Why? Because God loves you more than anything!

God Made Everything!

In the beginning God made from
nothing the heavens and the earth.

GENESIS 1:1

♥ ♥ ♥

In the beginning there was nothing but God. Then God started making things. He made the earth, the sky, the sun, twinkling stars, deep blue oceans, trees, flowers, people, animals—everything! God looked at all the wonderful things He made, and He said, "This is good!"

Are you near a window right now? Look outside. Everywhere you look there is something to see: people, places, and things. Can you name three things that God made?

Dear God, You must be very busy. There is so much
to see. Thank You, God, for everything! Amen.

A Very Special Son

*"For God so loved the world that He gave His only
Son. Whoever puts his trust in God's Son will not
be lost but will have life that lasts forever."*

JOHN 3:16

♥ ♥ ♥

You are your parents' son or daughter. God has a son, too. His name
is Jesus. God made a plan to send Jesus to earth as a baby boy
born to Mary and Joseph. When Jesus grew up, He did amazing
things. He taught people about God. He healed their sicknesses
and hurts. But, best of all, Jesus made a way for everybody to go
to heaven and live forever with God.

*Dear God, You must really love us to
want us to live with You forever in heaven.
I'm glad that You sent us Jesus! Amen.*

Look at Me. I'm Wonderful!

I praise you because you made me in an amazing and wonderful way. What you have done is wonderful. I know this very well.

PSALM 139:14 NCV

Do you know that God made you? He made you and every other child on earth. And when God made you, He knew exactly what to do. He chose the colors of your skin, eyes, and hair. He decided if you would be a boy or a girl. God even made a plan for every day of your life. When God made you, He made you in an amazing and wonderful way. He made you because He loves you.

Dear God, thank You for making me just the way I am. Amen.

Be Gentle

Let all people see how gentle you are.
The Lord is coming again soon.
PHILIPPIANS 4:5

♥ ♥ ♥

Puppies, kittens, and newborn babies—all of them need a gentle touch. Gentleness is the soft way you treat something. When you are gentle, you use quiet, kind words. You care about helping others feel safe and protected. Can you think of someone who is kind and gentle to you? Maybe you said, "Jesus." He is the kindest and gentlest of all.

Dear Jesus, You are always so gentle and kind to me. I want to be like You. Will You remind me to be gentle with others? Amen.

A Glad Heart

A glad heart is good medicine,
but a broken spirit dries up the bones.
PROVERBS 17:22

♥ ♥ ♥

Do you have a happy heart? God loves it when you are happy. He wants you always to feel cheerful and good. But God knows that sometimes His children feel sad, sick, hurt, or afraid. When that happens, we can ask God for help. God's love is like good medicine. He wants to make sad hearts glad again. So put on your best happy face. Do it right now! Let everyone see your big, happy heart.

Dear God, please help me to share my happy heart. Maybe if I smile and act happy, others will feel happy, too. Amen.

Peace!

"Blessed are the peacemakers, for they will be called children of God."

MATTHEW 5:9 NIV

♥ ♥ ♥

You are God's child. He loves you, and He wants you to pass His love along to others. One way of sharing God's love is to be a peacemaker. Peacemakers don't like to argue or fight. They help people to get along with one another. Peacemakers also help family members and friends find a little peace and quiet when they need it.

Are you a peacemaker? Do you know someone who would enjoy some peace and quiet today?

Dear God, I don't like to argue or fight. Help me to be a peacemaker, please. Amen.

GOD KNOWS ME!

"God knows how many hairs you have on your head."
LUKE 12:7

♥ ♥ ♥

God knows everything about you. He knows what you like and what you don't like. He knows and understands all your feelings. And He is with you all the time. God sees everything you do, and He hears every word you say. He even knows how many hairs are on your head right now. Isn't that amazing? Do you think you could count all those hairs? Yet God knows how many hairs are on every head of every person on earth!

Dear God, You know everything about everybody all the time. I think that's amazing. You are amazing, God. Amen.

Tell the Truth

O Lord, save me from lying lips and a false tongue.
PSALM 120:2

♥ ♥ ♥

A purple polka-dotted dragon stole my breakfast and ate my lunch and dinner! It's sure fun to make up stories sometimes! Storytelling is great when you're playing games and having fun. But it's also important to know when to tell the truth. You should never lie about things that you have really seen, heard, said, or done. Always be truthful with your parents and teachers. Will you ask God to help you?

Dear God, please help me to remember to tell the truth. Remind me that there is a right time and a wrong time for storytelling. Amen.

Jesus Loves Me

Jesus called the followers to Him and said,
"Let the little children come to Me."

LUKE 18:16

♥ ♥ ♥

Quick! Name all the people you can think of who love you. Wow. You are *so* loved! Do you know that Jesus loves you? He loves you with the greatest love of all. Jesus enjoyed being with kids. When He lived on earth, Jesus always invited children to come and spend time with Him. Jesus lives in heaven now. But you can still talk and spend time with Him every time you pray.

Hello, Jesus, it's me again. Thank You for
wanting to hear all about my day. Amen.

Jesus Is Always with Me

*"And I am with you always,
even to the end of the world."*

MATTHEW 28:20

♥ ♥ ♥

Can you think of a time when you are all alone? Maybe you are alone sometimes playing quietly in your room. Maybe you are alone when you are tucked into bed sleeping. But the truth is—you are never alone! Jesus is always with you. Everywhere you go, Jesus is there! You can be sure, because He promises not to leave you. And Jesus never, ever breaks a promise.

*Dear Jesus, I am thankful that
wherever I go and whatever I do,
You are always with me. Amen.*

The RoBBer

The robber comes only to steal and to kill and to destroy.
I came so they might have life, a great full life.

JOHN 10:10

♥ ♥ ♥

There is someone who wants to steal every good thing that God gives you. His name is Satan. He is a sneaky robber who wants you to do things that God doesn't want you to do. Keep your eyes open for him. If something doesn't feel right, stop and decide if it's Satan trying to get you to misbehave. Then ask Jesus to show you what to do.

> *Dear Jesus, please protect me from those*
> *things that Satan wants me to do. Amen.*

GoD's Loving–KinDness

The loving-kindness of God lasts all day long.

PSALM 52:1

♥ ♥ ♥

You are being kind if you care about others and go out of your way to be good to them. When you are gentle and play nice with your sister or brother—or even a dog, cat, or another pet, that's kindness, too. God loves it when His children are kind. Being loving and kind is important to God. His kindness lasts all day long, every day. Can you name a time when someone was kind to you?

> *Dear God, You are always so loving and kind to me.*
> *Will You help me, please, to be kind to others? Amen.*

I Forgive You

*"Forgive us our sins as we forgive
those who sin against us."*
MATTHEW 6:12

♥ ♥ ♥

When people do things that disobey God, it's called "sinning." Everybody sins sometimes. Humans are not perfect. But if we are sorry, God always forgives us. God wants you to be forgiving, too. Maybe someone said or did something that hurt your feelings or made you feel angry. Will you forgive that person right now? When people forgive, they make God happy.

*Dear God, I'm sorry for the wrong
things I do. Thank You for forgiving me,
and please help me to forgive others. Amen.*

God Is Always Right

"For I, the Lord, do not change."

MALACHI 3:6

♥ ♥ ♥

Has your mom or dad ever told you, "I changed my mind"? All people change their minds sometimes. Mind changing happens when we think about a choice we have made and decide that maybe it wasn't the best choice after all. God is different from people. God's choices are always right when He makes them. He never changes His mind. Everything He says and does is perfect all the time. God's decisions last forever.

Dear God, all of Your decisions are right. I know that I can always trust You not to change Your mind. Amen.

Perfectly Perfect God

God's way is perfect.

PSALM 18:30 NLT

♥ ♥ ♥

Perfect means that something has no mistakes. You might get a perfect score on a test. Your team might play a perfect soccer game. You might recite a Bible verse perfectly. But everything you do is not always perfect. Everyone makes mistakes sometimes—everyone except God. God is always perfect. He doesn't make mistakes, ever. God has never made a mistake, and He never will. That's why you can trust Him all the time to do what is best for you.

Dear God, I'm not perfect, but I'm glad that You are. Amen.

Be Respectful

Show respect for all people: Love the brothers and sisters of God's family, respect God, honor the king.

1 PETER 2:17 NCV

♥ ♥ ♥

Respect is a word that means showing good behavior. When you respect your parents and other grown-ups, you show that you trust them to know what is right and good for you. You can respect your friends by caring about their feelings and their things. You can also show respect for yourself by caring about how you look and act. And remember—always respect God. Obey and honor Him in everything you do.

Dear God, I will do my best to be respectful to everyone. I know You are proud of me when I show good manners. Amen.

GOD SEES ME!

"You are a God Who sees."
GENESIS 16:13

♥ ♥ ♥

God can do things that no human can do. For example, God is everywhere all at the same time. All at the same time, God sees everything that everyone does! Nobody knows how God can be everywhere and see everyone on earth. It's one of those things that only God knows.

Where are you right now? Wherever you go and whatever you do, remember that God sees you. Do your best to act in a way that makes Him proud.

Dear God, sometimes I forget that You are always watching me. Help me to remember that You see everything I do. Amen.

Light Up the World!

"You are the light of the world."

MATTHEW 5:14

♥ ♥ ♥

Do you know that you can help make the world a happy place? Jesus said you do that by sharing with others what you know about God. When you speak and act in ways pleasing to God, people will notice. When you talk with them about God, they will hear your words. Jesus said, "You are the light of the world." Be good, kind, and happy, and you will help make the world a brighter place.

Dear God, I want to help make the world a bright and happy place. Will You teach me how? Thank You, God. Amen.

Jesus Helps Me

I can do all things because Christ gives me the strength.
PHILIPPIANS 4:13

♥ ♥ ♥

When you read your Bible, you will see that sometimes Jesus is called "Christ," like in today's Bible verse. When something is not easy and you say, "I can't do that" or "I don't know how," the Bible says that Christ is ready to help. All you have to do is ask Jesus to help you be brave and strong when you face something new. He will change your "I can't" into a big "I can!"

Dear Christ Jesus, I know that You are always
with me, helping me to try new things. Thank You
for making me strong and brave. Amen.

Perfect Enough for Heaven

*"It will be that whoever calls on
the name of the Lord will be saved
from the punishment of sin."*

ACTS 2:21

♥ ♥ ♥

People are not perfect. We all mess up and do wrong things. Those mistakes are called "sin." There is no place in heaven for people who sin. But God wants us to live with Him in heaven, so He did something amazing. He sent His own Son, Jesus, to take the punishment we deserve for the wrong things we do. When Jesus did that, He made us perfect enough to live in heaven!

*Dear Jesus, wow, You really must love
us to take the punishment we deserve.
Thank You. I love You, too! Amen.*

Jesus Is My Teacher

*Let the teaching of Christ and
His words keep on living in you.*
COLOSSIANS 3:16

♥ ♥ ♥

Shhh, are you listening? You should always listen closely when people tell you about Jesus. You can learn all about Him by going to Sunday school and by reading the Bible, or by having someone read it to you. Jesus' words are very important. They teach you how to live right. Keep Jesus' words in your heart. Think about them all the time, and never let them go.

Dear Jesus, I'm listening. I want to hear Your words and learn from You. Thank You for being the best teacher ever. Amen.

Hooray for Today!

This is the day that the Lord has made.
Let us be full of joy and be glad in it.

PSALM 118:24

♥ ♥ ♥

Today is a special day. Today is special because God made it. This is the day that the Lord has made. Be joyful and be glad. God gave you this brand-new day to fill up with joy. So put a smile on your face—a big, big smile! Tell God, "Thank You for this fresh, new day." Hooray! Hooray! Hooray for today!

> *Dear God, thank You so much for this new day and for all the good things You have planned for it. Amen.*

With All My Heart

LORD, I will thank you with all my heart.

PSALM 138:1 NCV

♥ ♥ ♥

Your heart can be a little bit happy, or it can be all filled up with so much happiness that you want to jump for joy! Your heart can be a little bit sad, enough to make you grumpy, or your heart can be filled up with so much sadness that you cry. Now close your eyes. Think about all the wonderful things God does for you. Is your heart just a little bit thankful, or is it all filled up with thanks?

> *Dear God, when I think of You, my heart fills up with thankfulness. You are so good to me all the time. Amen.*

Dear God, I Love You

Loving God means to obey His Word,
and His Word is not hard to obey.

1 JOHN 5:3

♥ ♥ ♥

One way kids show their parents they love them is by trusting them and obeying their words. Do you know that God is like a parent? He is the Father to everyone, our heavenly Father. When you obey God, you show Him you love Him. If you think about how very much God loves you, His words are not hard to obey. Everything He says to us in the Bible is important because He cares so much for us. Tell God you love Him right now.

Dear God, I love You so much, and I
will show You by doing my best to
obey Your words. Amen.

I Can Always Trust God

Trust in the Lord with all your heart,
and do not trust in your own understanding.
PROVERBS 3:5

♥ ♥ ♥

Long ago, there was a man named Jonah who chose not to trust God. Instead of going where God told him to go, Jonah sailed off on a ship. He got caught in a storm and, *splash*, he was thrown into the ocean where, *gulp*, a big fish swallowed him up! God saved Jonah—*pffft*, the fish spit him out. Jonah's story reminds you to always trust God. He knows best. If you are not sure what God wants, ask Him. He will help you decide.

Dear God, I know that You love me, and I trust
You always to know what is best for me. Amen.

What Is a Christian?

They said to him, "Believe in the Lord Jesus and you will be saved—you and all the people in your house."
ACTS 16:31 NCV

♥ ♥ ♥

When you believe that Jesus took the punishment for your sins and you ask Jesus to come into your heart, a special part of Him comes and lives inside you. People who invite Jesus into their hearts are called Christians. You already know that another name for Jesus is Christ. The word *Christian* begins with Christ's name. *Christian* means: Christ in you. Isn't it awesome that Jesus wants to live inside your heart?

Dear Jesus, if I invite You to live in my heart, then You will be with me forever. I like that idea! Amen.

Moms and Dads

Children, as Christians, obey your parents.
This is the right thing to do.
EPHESIANS 6:1

♥ ♥ ♥

Do you know kids who disobey their mom or dad? Maybe you have disobeyed yours. There isn't one child on earth who hasn't disobeyed sometimes. But there is something that God wants all kids to remember: He put moms and dads on earth to be His helpers. He gave them the important job of teaching kids right from wrong. So do your best to obey your parents. God says it's the right thing to do.

Dear God, thank You for my mom and dad.
I promise to do my best to obey them. Amen.

Learn from the Ants

You lazy people can learn by watching an anthill.
PROVERBS 6:6 CEV

♥ ♥ ♥

If you look at an anthill, do you see a bunch of lazy ants sleeping or doing nothing? No! You see an army of ants going in and out of the anthill all day long. They work, carrying bits of sand to make the hill big and strong. They bring food into the hill. The ants are always doing something. The Bible says that we can learn from the ants to get up, get busy, and get things done.

Dear God, when I feel lazy, I will think
of the ants and get busy. Amen.

Amazing, Wonderful Me!

*I praise you because you made me in an amazing
and wonderful way. What you have done is
wonderful. I know this very well.*

PSALM 139:14 NCV

♥ ♥ ♥

Amazing and *wonderful*. Can you think of other words to describe something great? Maybe you said: *excellent, outstanding, awesome, cool!* All of those words can be used to describe the way God made you. God made you in a wonderful way, and He wants you to remember that all the time. Memorize today's Bible verse so you won't forget.

*Dear God, thank You for making me in a wonderful, amazing,
excellent, outstanding, awesome, and VERY COOL way! Amen.*

God's Plan for Me

"For I know the plans I have for you," says the Lord, "plans for well-being and not for trouble, to give you a future and a hope."

JEREMIAH 29:11

♥ ♥ ♥

God has great plans for you. He wants you to be happy, to stay out of trouble, and to be excited about your future. But there will be days when you feel unhappy. You might even get into trouble sometimes—you're not perfect, after all! If you feel a little nervous about the future, if you feel yourself not following God's plan, then ask Him to help you—He will!

Dear God, whenever I wander away from Your plan, please come and help me. Amen.

The Golden Rule

*"Do for other people what you would
like to have them do for you."*

LUKE 6:31

♥ ♥ ♥

Name one thing you have learned about God. Maybe you said,
"God is good." God always does good things for His children, and
God wants His children to do good things for others. Jesus gave
us the Golden Rule. It says, "Do for other people what you would
like to have them do for you." Will you do that? Will you follow
Jesus' rule and treat others the way you would like to be treated?
Be good, kind, and loving.

*Dear God, I will try hard to be good to others,
just like You are good to me. Amen.*

Do for other people what you would have them do for you.

HOW Great Is GOD?

You are as right and good as mountains are big.
You are as fair when You judge as a sea is deep.
PSALM 36:6

♥ ♥ ♥

How great is God? Imagine a mountain. Some mountains are so big that no one has climbed to the top. God's goodness could fill up even the biggest mountain. Now imagine an ocean. Some oceans are so deep that no one has reached the bottom. When God judges someone, His fairness could fill up the deepest ocean. God's greatness is greater than anything!

Dear God, You know what is on top of the biggest mountain and on the bottom of the deepest ocean. You are greater than anything on earth! Amen.

GOD KEEPS ME SAFE

*Of what great worth is Your loving-kindness, O God! The
children of men come and are safe in the shadow of Your wings.*
PSALM 36:7

♥ ♥ ♥

Newborn chicks snuggle safely under their mother's wings. When
they are old enough to come out and explore, they see a big world.
If something frightens them, what do you think they do? They run
back to their mama, and she covers them up with her big, safe wings.
The Bible says that God is like a mother bird that keeps her chicks
safe. You can count on Him, always, to protect you.

*Dear God, thank You for watching over
me and keeping me safe. Amen.*

I'll Give It a Try

For the Spirit God gave us does not make us timid, but gives us power, love and self-discipline.

2 TIMOTHY 1:7 NIV

♥ ♥ ♥

Timid is another word for shy. Maybe you are a little shy sometimes when you meet new people or try something new. That's okay! Everyone is shy sometimes. Today's Bible verse says that God helps us to be brave when we feel shy. His love gives us power to try new things and have good adventures. So the next time you feel timid, say, "I won't be shy, God. I'll give it a try!"

Dear God, whenever I feel timid, please help me to be brave. Amen.

This or That?

*Plans fail without good advice, but they
succeed with the advice of many others.*
PROVERBS 15:22 NCV

♥ ♥ ♥

Life is filled with choices. Some are little, like what kind of cereal to have for breakfast. Others are big, like choosing a special activity to do on your birthday. The Bible says that when you have a big decision to make, you should ask others for advice. Can you name two people you could ask? You should also ask God to help you decide. He knows the right answer all the time.

*Dear God, when I have trouble deciding what to do,
remind me to ask others for help. Amen.*

Do It with a Smile

*Be glad you can do the things you should be doing.
Do all things without arguing and talking about
how you wish you did not have to do them.*
PHILIPPIANS 2:14

♥ ♥ ♥

How do you act when Mom or Dad asks you to do something? Do you argue and wish you didn't have to? Everybody wishes they didn't have to do some things. But it's important to remember that God wants you to obey. Thank Him for giving you arms, legs, hands, feet, and a brain to get things done. Then put on a smile and get going.

*Dear God, please help me to obey my parents
and to be happy doing what they want. Amen.*

I Will Be Brave

When I am afraid, I will trust in You.

PSALM 56:3

♥ ♥ ♥

The Bible tells about a brave boy named David. Even when a whole army was afraid of a giant bully named Goliath, David stood up to that big guy and made him go away. David learned to be brave by trusting God to help.

You can be just like David. Whenever you feel afraid, you can say, "I won't be afraid, because I trust God to help me." Say it now: I won't be afraid, because I trust God to help me.

Dear God, I trust You. When I feel afraid, help me to remember that You love me and will protect me. Amen.

The One and Only God

"Have no other gods except Me."
DEUTERONOMY 5:7

♥ ♥ ♥

The Bible tells stories about people who bowed down to golden statues as if those statues were God. It tells about kings who acted like gods and wanted their subjects to kneel before them. When the real God saw these things, it made Him very unhappy and angry, too. There is only one God, and He knows you. He made you, and He loves you all the time. Nothing should be more important to you than Him.

Dear God, I know that You are the one and only God. Nobody else can do what You do. You are the greatest! Amen.

Good Friends

*Walk with the wise and become wise;
associate with fools and get in trouble.*
PROVERBS 13:20 NLT

♥ ♥ ♥

Name three of your friends. Now say something you like about each one. You probably didn't say, "I like that my friend gets me into trouble." It's no fun to be friends with someone who leads you to do what is wrong. That's why the Bible reminds us to be careful when choosing friends. Good friends help each other follow the rules. Are you that kind of friend?

*Dear God, thank You for good friends.
Please help me to be a good friend, too. Amen.*

NOBODY IS PERFECT

*For all men have sinned and have missed
the shining-greatness of God.*
ROMANS 3:23

♥ ♥ ♥

If someone is perfect, it means that person
has never made a mistake. No one on earth
is perfect, not anyone who is alive right now
or has ever lived—except Jesus. Jesus is the
only one who has ever lived a perfect life.
Everyone makes mistakes. That's why Jesus
came. He erased our mistakes, just as if they
never happened. If you believe that, then when
you go to heaven someday you will be perfect
like Him.

*Dear God, I'm not perfect. I make
mistakes. But when I tell You "I'm sorry,"
I know You will forgive me. Amen.*

GOD LOVES ME!

We love Him because He loved us first.

1 JOHN 4:19

♥ ♥ ♥

Many people love you, but who was the *first* to love you? Maybe you said your mom or dad. But someone else was first. God! He has loved you forever. You were always on His mind. He loved you when He made you. Then He sent you to earth to be loved even more. God just keeps pouring His love all over you. Open your arms up wide like you are giving God a big hug. Tell Him how much you love Him.

Dear God, my heart is all filled up with love for You. I love You so much! Amen.

BiBle-wise

My child, if you are wise, then I will be happy.
PROVERBS 23:15 NCV

♥ ♥ ♥

You might be smart, but are you wise? Smart means you study hard and get good grades. Wise means you understand how to be kind, get along with others, and live right. The Bible has all the information you need to become wise. The Bible is God's big book of learning. As you learn more from God about living, you will become wise like Jesus. He is the wisest of all!

Dear God, I want to learn from You to be wise like Jesus.
Will You help me, please? Amen.

Be Gentle and Kind

*"You must have loving-kindness just as
your Father has loving-kindness."*

LUKE 6:36

♥ ♥ ♥

If a puppy played too rough and hurt you, what would you do? Would you be kind and gentle while showing the puppy what it had done wrong? When people hurt God by doing something wrong, God doesn't hurt them back or turn them away. God corrects them in a kind, gentle way. That's what He wants you to do. He wants you always to be kind and gentle, just the way He is.

*Dear God, I want to be more like You—kind, loving, and gentle—
even when someone hurts my feelings. Amen.*

My Best Friend

*Keep your minds thinking about
things in heaven. Do not think
about things on the earth.*
COLOSSIANS 3:2

♥ ♥ ♥

How often do you think about God? When you play, do you say, "Isn't this fun, God?" or when you enjoy a special treat, "Thank You, God, this is so good!" God never stops thinking about you. He wants to be your best friend. You can have a friendship with God by thinking about Him all day and by talking with Him about everything you do. What would you like to tell Him today?

*Dear God, thank You for being my best friend.
I want us to do everything together. Amen.*

Dear God. . .

*"You must not use the name of the LORD your God thoughtlessly;
the LORD will punish anyone who misuses his name."*

EXODUS 20:7 NCV

♥ ♥ ♥

God's name is special. Think about it: Do you know anyone else named God? God's name is just for Him. When you say His name, it's like saying a prayer. Some people disrespect God's name. They use it like a swear word, and that is very wrong. You should only say things like "Oh God" or "Dear God" when you are talking with Him.

*Dear God, I will always be respectful when using
Your name. I will say it like a prayer. Amen.*

That Doesn't Belong to You!

"Do not steal."

EXODUS 20:15

♥ ♥ ♥

Have you taken something from a family member or friend without asking? Maybe that person said, "Hey! That doesn't belong to you." And you said, "I was just borrowing it." When you borrow something without asking first, it's the same as stealing. It doesn't matter if the something you borrow is small or big. It doesn't belong to you. One of God's special rules is: "Do not steal." So, before you borrow something, always remember to ask.

*Dear God, I'm sorry for the times I've forgotten to ask.
Next time I will try to remember. Amen.*

It's True!

Every word of God has been proven true.
He is a safe-covering to those who trust in Him.

PROVERBS 30:5

♥ ♥ ♥

You should always tell the truth, because then people will believe they can trust you. Trust is important. When others trust you, they know for sure they can count on you. Who do you trust? Did you say, "God"? God is someone you can trust all the time. Everything He says is true. He has never told a lie, and He never will.

Dear God, I trust You, and I want You to trust me, too.
Help me, please, to always tell the truth. Amen.

Honor Your Mom and Dad

"Honor your father and your mother,
as the Lord your God has told you."

DEUTERONOMY 5:16

♥ ♥ ♥

God says to honor your mom and dad. That means you follow their rules and don't talk back. It also means you are there for your parents when they need you. You can show honor by helping with chores without complaining and also by giving Mom and Dad peace and quiet when they need it. Jesus is an awesome example of someone who honored His Father. He was respectful and always did what His Father asked.

Dear Jesus, I want to be like You. I promise to do
my best to honor my parents all the time. Amen.

Hard as Rock

*"Trust in the Lord forever. For the
Lord God is a Rock that lasts forever."*

ISAIAH 26:4

♥ ♥ ♥

Can you name things made from rock? Maybe
you live in a brick house. Bricks are rocks. So
are most roads and sidewalks. Sand is billions
of tiny rocks. Mountains can be made of rock,
too. Hold a rock in your hand. It feels hard
doesn't it? Like it could last forever. God is
like that hard, strong rock. He will live forever.
He is unbreakable, and nothing can hurt Him.

*Dear God, I like knowing that You are forever
and that I can trust You to protect me. Amen.*

GOD the creator

*But LORD, you are our father. We are like clay,
and you are the potter; your hands made us all.*
ISAIAH 64:8 NCV

♥ ♥ ♥

Do you enjoy making things? God does. God is like someone who makes beautiful artwork from clay. But instead of using clay, God has His own secret way of making things. After He made you, God sent you to earth because He wanted the whole world to see one of His most special creations—His perfectly wonderful you!

*Dear God, I like knowing that You made me.
I think everything You make is beautiful. Amen.*

"Hey! That's Mine."

"Do not steal."
DEUTERONOMY 5:19

♥ ♥ ♥

If someone grabbed your favorite toy and ran away with it, that would be stealing. You might say, "Hey! That's mine." It's no fun having someone take something that belongs to you. That's why God made a rule: "Do not steal." Whether it's something important, like your favorite toy, or something small, like a piece of candy, don't take it without asking. When you respect other people's things, then you make God happy.

Dear God, I know that stealing is wrong, and I promise never to take something that doesn't belong to me. Amen.

Inside My Heart

Do you not know that your body is a house of God where the Holy Spirit lives? God gave you His Holy Spirit. Now you belong to God. You do not belong to yourselves.

1 CORINTHIANS 6:19

♥ ♥ ♥

You already know that God is everywhere all the time. But do you know that He lives inside your body? God's Spirit is inside your heart. He is the God person who helps you with whatever you do. No one, not even a doctor, can see God inside you, because He's invisible! Remember to keep your body healthy and clean so it's a nice place for God to live.

Dear God, I promise to do my best to take good care of my body. Amen.

My Heavenly Body

Our body is like a house we live in here on earth. When it is destroyed, we know that God has another body for us in heaven. . . . This body will last forever.

2 CORINTHIANS 5:1

♥ ♥ ♥

When Jesus went back to heaven, He had a new body—one that would never die. Jesus' follower John saw Jesus in His new body. He wore a long coat that came to His feet and a gold belt around His chest. When you go to heaven one day, you will have a new body, too. You and your new body will last forever.

Dear God, thank You for having a forever plan for my body. Amen.

The Ten Commandments

"So keep My Laws and obey them. I am the Lord."

LEVITICUS 22:31

♥ ♥ ♥

God gives us ten special rules called the Ten Commandments.
1. Love God more than anything.
2. Make God more important than everything else.
3. Respect God's name.
4. Take one day to rest and honor God.
5. Obey your parents.
6. Don't hurt anyone.
7. Married people should respect each other.
8. Don't steal.
9. Never lie.
10. Don't be jealous of what others have.

Can you remember them all?

*Dear God, I will remember Your rules,
and I will try to obey them all the time. Amen.*

Faith—Big and Strong

The Lord will give strength to His people.
PSALM 29:11

♥ ♥ ♥

Show off your muscles! When you were a tiny baby, you were so weak you couldn't even lift up your head. Now you have muscles strong enough to lift books, toys, and so many other things you couldn't carry a few years ago. Every day, God is helping your body to grow. He is also growing your faith. Remember—faith means trusting God. Keep on trusting Him, and by the time you are all grown up your faith will be big and strong.

Dear God, I trust You. I want my faith to get bigger and stronger every day. Amen.

count the Stars

He knows the number of the stars.
He gives names to all of them.

PSALM 147:4

♥ ♥ ♥

Do this with your family: go outside some night and try counting the stars. Spend five minutes counting and naming as many stars as you can. When the five minutes are over, see if you can remember each star and its name. Was it easy or hard to remember them all? God is so great that He knows exactly how many stars are in the sky. He even named each one!

Dear God, You made all those stars, and You
know all their names. You're the greatest! Amen.

Little Kids, Big Things

*The true children of God are those
who let God's Spirit lead them.*
ROMANS 8:14 NCV

♥ ♥ ♥

Five thousand people had sat for hours listening to Jesus teach. Jesus knew that they needed lunch, but He had nothing to give them. A little boy in the crowd had five loaves of bread and two fish. What good would that do? Still, he decided to share his lunch with Jesus. And do you know what Jesus did? Somehow, He made that boy's lunch into enough to feed everyone—with leftovers! When little people trust Jesus, He helps them do great things.

*Dear Jesus, You are amazing! I want to be Your helper.
Will You show me how? Amen.*

Animals, Animals, Animals!

Then God made the wild animals of the earth after their kind, and the cattle after their kind, and every thing that moves upon the ground after its kind. And God saw that it was good.

GENESIS 1:25

♥ ♥ ♥

Some of God's animals are huge! In the Bible, God says He made the hippopotamus with legs like iron, strong and powerful. He gave the crocodile thick skin and sharp teeth that lock tight on anything that gets near its mouth. People might be afraid of those big animals, but God isn't. He's not afraid of anything. God says He plays with the crocodile as if it's a bird! Which of God's animals is your favorite?

Dear God, thank You for making all kinds of animals. Amen.

Be Careful What You Say

"If only you would be altogether silent!
For you, that would be wisdom."

JOB 13:5 NIV

♥ ♥ ♥

Have you ever said something that got you
into trouble? Everyone does it sometimes.
They don't mean to say unkind things or hurt
feelings. But it happens. Memorize today's
Bible verse. It will help you to think before
you speak. Sometimes it's best to say nothing
at all. Choose your words wisely. That way,
everything you say will be good and kind.

Dear God, will You remind me, please,
to think about my words before I say them?
I don't want to hurt anyone's feelings. Amen.

What Smells So Good?

We are a sweet smell of Christ that reaches up to God.

2 CORINTHIANS 2:15

♥ ♥ ♥

Quick! Name three things that smell good. God created those wonderful smells. The Bible describes some of God's best-smelling creations. The wise men brought perfume and spices for Baby Jesus. King Solomon said that his wife's breath smelled like apples. Jacob described his son's clothing as smelling like a field—in a good way! The Bible even tells how we smell to God. Our scent is perfectly sweet and wonderful, like Jesus!

Dear God, whenever I smell something good,
I will think of You. Amen.

How Does God Do That?

"Hear this, O Job. Stop and think about the great
works of God. Do you know how God does them,
and makes the lightning shine from His cloud?"

JOB 37:14–15

♥ ♥ ♥

Could you be everywhere at the same time? If someone asked you to create a person or a puppy or kitten, could you do it? Would a storm obey you if you told it to stop? God can do all that and so much more. No one knows how God does the amazing things He does. That's what makes Him so great. He does things that no man, woman, or child could ever do!

Dear God, I think You are awesome,
and I'm happy that You are my God. Amen.

Talking with God

Never stop praying.
1 THESSALONIANS 5:17

♥ ♥ ♥

When you pray, you are talking with God. You kneel down before you sleep and say your prayers. You say prayers in Sunday school and church, too. But do you know that you can talk with God all day long? You don't have to be kneeling or in church to pray. You can talk with God wherever you are and while you are doing other things. God is always listening. He even hears when you think prayers instead of saying them out loud.

Dear God, I like that You want me to talk with You all the time.
Thank You for never being too busy to listen. Amen.

Wind, Wind, Go Away!

He got up and spoke sharp words to the wind.
He said to the sea, "Be quiet! Be still." At once the
wind stopped blowing. There were no more waves.

MARK 4:39

♥ ♥ ♥

Whooosh! A great wind blew across the sea. Big waves rocked the boat Jesus and His disciples were in. *Swoosh!* Water splashed inside the boat, and the disciples were afraid. "Jesus! We are all going to die," they cried. But Jesus knew better. He told the wind, "Be still!" And the wind stopped blowing. Nothing is more powerful than Jesus. Even the wind obeys Him.

Dear Jesus, whenever something makes me afraid,
I know that I can count on You. Thank You! Amen.

I Believe

Now faith is being sure we will get what we hope for.
It is being sure of what we cannot see.

HEBREWS 11:1

♥ ♥ ♥

Take a big, deep breath. Let it out slowly. Can you see the air going in and out of your mouth? Air is something you cannot see, but it's there. You know it because you need air to stay alive. God is like air. You can't see Him, but you need Him and He is always with you. Faith means believing for sure that God is there. Do you believe?

Dear God, I have faith that You are with
me all the time. I believe in You! Amen.

TOUCH JESUS

*They begged Him that they might touch
the bottom of His coat. As many as touched
the bottom of His coat were healed.*

MATTHEW 14:36

♥ ♥ ♥

When Jesus lived on earth, people saw the amazing things He did. Wherever He went, Jesus healed sick people. Just by reaching out and touching His coat, people were healed. Did you know that you can still touch Jesus? You can't touch Him with your hands, but you can touch Him with your heart. You do it by talking with Him in prayer. Touch Him right now. Say a little Jesus prayer.

*Hi, Jesus. It's me, just reaching out to touch
You with my heart. I love You! Amen.*

LOOK UP!

Lift up your eyes and look to the heavens:
Who created all these?
ISAIAH 40:26 NIV

♥ ♥ ♥

Look up at the sky, but don't look right at the sun; it can hurt your eyes. Look up at the clouds and the color of the sky. Look up at night and see the moon and stars. Who made the sky and everything in it? God did! His sky is so big that we can't see it all—not even with the most powerful telescopes. We can only imagine what is up there.

Dear God, I wonder what is beyond the stars. Whatever it is,
I know it's wonderful because You made it. Amen.

Solomon

*Now, O Lord my God, You have made Your servant king
in place of my father David. But I am only a little child.
I do not know how to start or finish.*

1 KINGS 3:7

♥ ♥ ♥

Long ago, there was a boy named Solomon not much older than you
are now. When Solomon's dad, King David, died, it was Solomon's
turn to be king. "I'm only a child," Solomon told God. "I don't even
know how to start being a king!" God helped Solomon. He taught
Solomon what to do from start to finish.

*Dear God, when I don't know how to start something new,
I will trust You to help me. Amen.*

It's Too Heavy!

"For My way of carrying a load is
easy and My load is not heavy."

MATTHEW 11:30

♥ ♥ ♥

Have you tried to pick up a dog or even another child and said, "Too heavy!" Some things are too big for a child to carry. Worries can feel big and heavy, too. When you worry, it feels like everything is bigger and stronger than you. But you don't have to feel that way. Jesus says you should ask Him to pick up your worries and carry them away. Jesus is very strong. He knows just what to do. So let Him carry your worries for you.

Dear Jesus, please come to me when I
worry and take my worries away. Amen.

In God's Hand

*"In His hand is the life of every living
thing and the breath of all men."*

JOB 12:10

♥ ♥ ♥

God doesn't care just about people; He cares for every living thing. God watches over all the animals on earth, all the fish in the sea, the birds and bugs, even the grass, trees, and flowers. God made and cares for everything that is alive. Here is something to think about today: God is so big that every living thing can fit in the palm of His hand!

Dear God, thank You for watching over all the animals, every living thing, and especially me. Amen.

First in Line

"You have not chosen Me, I have chosen you."

JOHN 15:16

♥ ♥ ♥

Imagine being chosen first in line for something good or being chosen first to be on someone's team. It feels good to be first, doesn't it? Do you know that God will always choose you first? You are so special to Him that when You come to Him, He always and forever wants you first in line. Whenever you pray, whatever you need, God says, "Come to Me, little one. I'm right here waiting for you."

Dear God, I love knowing that I always come first with You. Amen.

Jesus Is My Best Friend

God is faithful. He chose you to be joined
together with His Son, Jesus Christ our Lord.
1 CORINTHIANS 1:9

♥ ♥ ♥

Who are your best friends? God chose them for you. He also chose
your very best friend. Do you know who that is? It's Jesus! God
chose Jesus to be your friend above all other friends. Jesus is the
perfect friend. You can trust Him with everything. He will never let
you down. And He will stay your best friend forever—even when
you are all grown up.

Dear God, thank You for choosing Jesus to be my very
best friend. I love Him, and He loves me, too. Amen.

Sing to the Lord

Sing to the Lord a new song.
Let all the earth sing to the Lord.
PSALM 96:1

♥ ♥ ♥

God loves it when you sing. It doesn't matter if you sing well or
not. To God's ears, your singing voice is beautiful music. God
especially likes it when His kids make up new songs to sing to
Him. Can you do that right now? Make up a little song to sing to
the Lord. It doesn't have to be perfect. Just sing a little song and
tell God you love Him.

Dear God, I will praise You with singing. Every day,
I will try to remember to sing You a little song. Amen.

Friendly Advice

*The sweet smell of perfume and
oils is pleasant, and so is good
advice from a friend.*
PROVERBS 27:9 NCV

♥ ♥ ♥

You might not always know the right thing
to do. When you aren't sure, you can ask for
advice from your parents, teachers, and friends.
The Bible verses you have learned and stories
from the Bible can also help you decide. And,
of course, you should always tell God when
you don't know what to do. He has the best
advice of all.

*Dear God, when I'm not sure about something,
please remind me to ask for help. Amen.*

Quiet, Please

Be quiet and know that I am God.
PSALM 46:10

♥ ♥ ♥

"I can't hear you!" The world is so loud sometimes that all you hear is noise. If someone had something important to say, you might not hear. God says, "Be quiet and know that I am God," because He wants you to spend time with Him listening. Tonight, lie quietly in bed and see if God fills your head with good thoughts. That is how God speaks to us sometimes, by putting His thoughts into our heads when we are alone and quiet with Him.

Here I am, God, alone with You and listening.
Is there something You want to tell me? Amen.

Do What Is Right

My dear friend, do not follow what is bad;
follow what is good. The one who does good
belongs to God. But the one who does evil
has never known God.
3 JOHN 1:11 NCV

♥ ♥ ♥

You know in your heart the difference between right and wrong. God put that knowing there. When you are faced with doing something wrong, God's voice in your heart says, *"Don't do that."* When you hear His voice, listen and obey. Don't let anyone trick you into doing what is wrong. Always choose what is right.

Dear God, help me, please, always to listen
for Your voice and do what is right. Amen.

I'm Sorry

*Tell your sins to each other. And pray for each other
so you may be healed. The prayer from the heart
of a man right with God has much power.*

JAMES 5:16

♥ ♥ ♥

When you hurt someone's feelings or do something wrong, do you always say "I'm sorry"? Those two little words are very important to God. They show that you care about others. Get into the habit of saying "I'm sorry." And remember—you can always tell God when you've messed up, and He will forgive you.

*Dear God, I will try to remember to say "I'm sorry" whenever
I hurt someone or do something I know is wrong. Amen.*

Jesus Changes My Heart

*This means that anyone who belongs to Christ has become
a new person. The old life is gone; a new life has begun!*

2 CORINTHIANS 5:17 NLT

♥ ♥ ♥

Something wonderful happens when you ask Jesus to come into your heart. He wipes away all the wrong things you have ever done. It's like they never happened. Jesus gives you a clean heart that's ready to be filled up with Him. No human can do that. It takes Jesus' superpower! Have you asked Him to come into your heart?

*Jesus, You are the only one who can wipe away my
sins and give me a clean heart. I love You! Amen.*

GOD, Bless My Family

*"Please, bless my family. Let it continue
before you always. Lord GOD, you have said so.
With your blessing let my family always be blessed."*
2 Samuel 7:29 NCV

♥ ♥ ♥

God doesn't just plunk His children down on earth and forget about them. He puts His kids in families. Families come in all shapes and sizes. Some are big. Some are small. Some have two parents and others one. God wants everyone in a family to get along—moms, dads, sisters, brothers, grandparents, aunts, uncles, cousins—everyone! God watches over His families. Will you ask Him to bless yours today?

*Dear God, thank You for my family. Bless us,
please, and help us all to get along. Amen.*

Dear Father, I Need. . .

*And my God will give you everything you need
because of His great riches in Christ Jesus.*

PHILIPPIANS 4:19

♥ ♥ ♥

Another name for God is heavenly Father. God made everyone, so He is the Father of all. Your heavenly Father is the best! He loves you, and He knows exactly what you need all the time. Think about the things you need every day. Food, water, clothes. What else? God provides those things. Will you remember to thank Him every day for giving you what you need?

*Dear God, You are such a good heavenly Father!
Thank You for providing everything I need. Amen.*

I Saw a Tyrannosaurus!

"Do not tell a lie about your neighbor."
DEUTERONOMY 5:20

♥ ♥ ♥

What if you ran to your mom and said, "I just saw Mr. Jones, next door, drive away with a tyrannosaurus in his car!" Your mom would know you were telling a lie. A tyrannosaurus is a dinosaur, and it could never fit in your neighbor's car. One of God's special rules is to always tell the truth. It's fun to make up stories about pretend people, but you should never make up stories about real people—your neighbors or anyone else.

Dear God, I will tell the truth about people all the time. Amen.

GOD HEARS ME

*I will cry out and complain in the evening and morning
and noon, and He will hear my voice.*

PSALM 55:17

♥ ♥ ♥

Do you know that God hears all your words? Think about that.
He hears every word, good and bad. God hears when you say nice
things to and about others. He hears when you complain. When
you cry, God hears, and He hears when you pray. Even when you
think words in your head, God hears them. So do your best today
and every day to say and think good things.

*Dear God, I will do my best to choose good words.
And thank You, God, for hearing when I pray. Amen.*

Jeremiah

*Then I said, "O, Lord God! I do not
know how to speak. I am only a boy."*
JEREMIAH 1:6

♥ ♥ ♥

God gave an important job to a boy named Jeremiah. He told Jeremiah, "I want you to tell everyone what I have to say." Jeremiah was afraid. "But, God, I am only a boy! I don't know how to give speeches." God said to Jeremiah, "Don't be afraid. I will give you the words."

Is there something you are afraid to do? Remember Jeremiah. Trust God to show you the way.

*Dear God, when I am afraid to do something,
please remind me of how You helped Jeremiah. Amen.*

Angels, Angels Everywhere!

*"Do you not think that I can pray to
My Father? At once He would send
Me more than 70,000 angels."*

MATTHEW 26:53

♥ ♥ ♥

Jesus said He could ask God to send angels
and God would send them right away. Not just
one angel or two but more than 70,000! That's
a lot of angels. God's angels are all around. You
can't see them, but they are there. You can be
like Jesus and ask God to send His angels to
watch over you. Would you like to do that now?

*Dear God, I like knowing that Your angels
are all around. Will You send some to
watch over me, please? Amen.*

Jesus Always Loves Me

*Nothing above us, nothing below us, nor anything else
in the whole world will ever be able to separate us from
the love of God that is in Christ Jesus our Lord.*

ROMANS 8:39 NCV

♥ ♥ ♥

Jesus loves you with a special forever love. He promises that nothing
in the whole world will ever take His love away. If you mess up and
do something you know you shouldn't, Jesus will still love you. If
you move to a new house or go on a vacation, Jesus will go along
so He can love you wherever you are. Now that's true love!

*Dear Jesus, wow, You must really, really love me!
I love You, too. Amen.*

God's Son, Jesus

*The Child grew and became strong in spirit. He was filled
with wisdom and the loving-favor of God was on Him.*

LUKE 2:40

♥ ♥ ♥

The Bible has many examples of God using kids to do important
things. Think about Jesus. God sent Him to earth as a baby. Jesus
learned and grew up to do God's greatest job of all—He saved the
world from sin. If you think you are too young or too little to do
God's work, remember the kids from the Bible. God helped them
grow up, and He will help you, too.

*Dear God, I might be a child, but I can do
great things when I trust in You. Amen.*

First and Last

The Lord God says, "I am the First and the Last,
the beginning and the end of all things. I am the All-
powerful One Who was and Who is and Who is to come."
REVELATION 1:8

♥ ♥ ♥

It's fun to be first, isn't it? But sometimes last is good, too. God is both first and last! He existed first before anything else. Someday God will be done with this earth, and He will make new heavens and a new earth for all of His people. God will be the last one to see this earth before He creates a new one.

Dear God, You have everything all planned out,
for now and forever. I love You! Amen.

GOD Wants GooD Things for Me

We know that God makes all things work together for the good
of those who love Him and are chosen to be a part of His plan.

ROMANS 8:28

♥ ♥ ♥

Maybe you prayed for something but you didn't get what you prayed for. Or maybe something made you sad, and you said, "God, why did You let that happen?" The truth is that you can't always know why God does some things. But you can count on this: God never, ever messes up. Even better, He promises always to work things out for good for those who love Him.

Dear God, I don't always understand, but I know that
You love me and only want good things for me. Amen.

Praise the LorD!

Let all things praise the name of the LORD,
because they were created at his command.

PSALM 148:5 CEV

♥ ♥ ♥

A psalm is a kind of poem. The Bible has a whole book of psalms. Many of them say to praise God. Praise means telling God that He is very great. One of the Bible poets said that everything God created should praise Him. Everything in the sky—the sun, moon, and stars. Everything on earth—animals, weather, mountains, oceans. And especially people—like you! Can you praise God right now? Tell Him how great you think He is.

Dear God, I praise You because You are the greatest of all! Amen.

Jesus Makes Me Strong

Let the weakling say, "I am strong!"
JOEL 3:10 NIV

♥ ♥ ♥

When you see a grown-up lift something really heavy, you might think, *I couldn't lift that even if I tried.* But that doesn't mean you are weak. Real strength isn't about muscles. It's about trusting Jesus. When you trust Jesus, then He will help you stand up to any problem that gets in your way. With Jesus on your side, you'll be superstrong! And with His help, you'll knock that problem down.

Dear Jesus, I trust You, and I want You on my side. Whatever gets in my way, please help me to be strong. Amen.

More Faith, Please

"Lord, I have faith. Help my weak faith to be stronger!"
MARK 9:24

♥ ♥ ♥

Do you know what faith is? Faith is believing that God loves you. It is believing that God will always help you and He will keep every promise He makes. Faith can be hard sometimes, especially when God wants you to wait. If you aren't careful, your faith can become weak. It might even slip away altogether. When you feel your faith getting smaller, ask God for more. Memorize the above Bible verse, and use it as your prayer.

Dear Lord, "I have faith. Help my weak faith to be stronger!" Amen.

Jesus Is My Shady Spot

The LORD guards you. The LORD is the shade
that protects you from the sun.
PSALM 121:5 NCV

♥ ♥ ♥

Do you enjoy a shady spot on a hot, sunny summer day? The shade feels cooler. And shade helps protect your skin from sunburn. The Bible says that Jesus is like a shady place on a sunny day. Being in His company it always feels better. And Jesus is the best protector ever! He protects you from all kinds of hurts. So the next time you enjoy a shady spot on a sunny day, think of Jesus. He's right there with you.

Dear Jesus, being with you feels good.
Thanks for being my protector. Amen.

Make a Joyful Noise

Make a joyful noise unto the LORD, all ye lands.
PSALM 100:1 KJV

♥ ♥ ♥

God loves it when His people make happy sounds to praise Him. Praise is a word that means "thanking God for His greatness." Some people praise God by singing to Him. Others use musical instruments to play songs for Him. In church, people might shout, "Hallelujah!" or "Praise God!" What are the happiest sounds you can think of? Make a joyful noise to the Lord! Tell Him how much you love Him.

Dear God, I praise You because I know You are so good.
There is no one as good as You! Amen.

Hide-and-Seek

I love those who love me, and those who seek me find me.
PROVERBS 8:17 NIV

♥ ♥ ♥

Playing hide-and-seek is fun. Some kids are so good at hiding that you think you will never find them. There is someone who is not at all good at playing hide-and-seek. Do you know who it is? It's God! He says that when you look for Him, you will always find Him. God loves you, and He will never hide from you.

Dear God, You might not be fun to play hide-and-seek with, but that's okay. I like knowing that You are always with me. Amen.

Will You Be My Helper?

Two people are better than one,
because they get more done by working together.
ECCLESIASTES 4:9 NCV

♥ ♥ ♥

Maybe you and your family work together doing chores around the house. You get more done when two or more people work together. Sometimes finding a helper is easy. But if you have to work alone, remember this: Jesus is your Helper. He is always with you. You can talk with Him while you work. And you can ask Him to help you do your best work.

Dear Jesus, will You be my helper? Work is
more fun when I'm talking with You. Amen.

God Doesn't Change

Every good action and every perfect gift is from God. These
good gifts come down from the Creator of the sun, moon,
and stars, who does not change like their shifting shadows.
JAMES 1:17 NCV

♥ ♥ ♥

Have you watched a puppy grow up and become a dog? Every living thing changes. You will, too. You will change not only in the way you look but also in the ways you think and act. There is someone who will never change. Do you know who? It's God! Everything He is and does is good and perfect—always and forever.

Dear God, please remind me that You won't change.
You will always be the one I can count on. Amen.

Jesus Knows My Name

When Jesus came by, he looked up at Zacchaeus and
called him by name. "Zacchaeus!" he said. "Quick,
come down! I must be a guest in your home today."
LUKE 19:5 NLT

♥ ♥ ♥

Jesus was walking with a big crowd when He saw a man up in a tree looking down at Him. The man had never met Jesus. He climbed the tree just to get a better look at Him. Jesus stopped walking. "Zacchaeus!" He said. Why did Jesus know that man's name? Because He knows everyone's name. Jesus knows your name, too!

Dear Jesus, You must really love me! You know
my name and everything about me. Amen.

I'm so Angry!

The Lord is slow to anger
and great in power.
NAHUM 1:3

♥ ♥ ♥

"Ooooh, I'm so mad!" A temper tantrum is like blowing up a balloon. If you put too much air inside, it explodes with a great big *POP*! It's no fun getting angry. Anger makes you and everyone around you feel bad. God is the best example of someone who is slow to get angry. He is very patient when He is upset. Whenever you feel your temper blowing up inside you, will you try to be more like Him?

Dear God, when I feel angry,
will You help me, please, to be patient
and calm? Thank You. Amen.

The Best Thing I Ever Ate

O taste and see that the Lord is good.
How happy is the man who trusts in Him!
PSALM 34:8

♥ ♥ ♥

What is the best thing you ever ate? Think about how good it tasted. It made you want even more, didn't it? That's how good God is. As soon as you feel a little of His love, you want more and more and more! But God isn't like an ice-cream sundae that's gone too soon. He has plenty of goodness for everyone. Enough to last forever.

Dear God, You are so good to me. You are like a special treat that I can eat all day every day. I think You are great! Amen.

A Special Message for Kids

How can a young person live a pure life?
By obeying your word.

PSALM 119:9 NCV

♥ ♥ ♥

You are learning about God! Can you name three things you know about Him? Today God has a special message for you. He wants you to obey His words in the Bible. The Bible is filled with God's words about how He wants you to live. Get in the habit of reading your children's Bible, or ask a grown-up to read to you from the Bible. Then practice the things you learn.

Dear God, I'm learning to know You better!
Thank You for speaking to me through
Your Bible. Amen.

Be Like Jesus

The one who says he belongs to Christ should
live the same kind of life Christ lived.
1 JOHN 2:6

♥ ♥ ♥

The Bible is sixty-six smaller books put together to make one big book. Many of the smaller books are named for the people who wrote them. Look in the Bible for books named Matthew, Mark, Luke, and John. These books will teach you about Jesus! As you learn about Jesus, try to be like Him. If you practice the ways Jesus acted around other people, God will be pleased with you.

Dear God, I want to learn all about Jesus.
Will You show me how to be more like Him? Amen.

Perfect Peace

You will keep in perfect peace all who trust in you,
all whose thoughts are fixed on you!
ISAIAH 26:3 NLT

♥ ♥ ♥

Peace means feeling that you are safe and all right. Perfect peace is when you feel safe and all right all the time. God wants you to have perfect peace. He says that if you always keep your mind on Him and trust Him, you will be perfectly peaceful because you know He is with you. Do you think about God all day long?

Dear God, I want perfect peace. Please help me
keep my mind on You and trust You. Amen.

GOD's Great Love

*See what great love the Father has for
us that He would call us His children.*

1 JOHN 3:1

♥ ♥ ♥

Who loves you? Maybe you said your mom, dad, or another family member. You are right. They love you so much! Their love for you is bigger than almost anything. But there is one who loves you even more. Do you know who? It's God! His love for you is bigger than any person's love. His love for you is the greatest love of all. You are His precious, wonderful child—and oh, how He loves you!

Dear God, I feel so loved! I love You, too. Amen.

We Are God's People

*"People look at the outside of a person,
but the LORD looks at the heart."*

1 SAMUEL 16:7 NCV

♥ ♥ ♥

Some people are short.
Some people are tall.
Some are big and others small!

People come in all shapes and sizes with different colors of skin, eyes, and hair. But everyone is the same in one important way. Can you guess what it is? God made them all! It doesn't matter to God how a person looks on the outside, and it shouldn't matter to you either. God cares that His people act with kind and loving hearts.

*Dear God, thank You for reminding me to make up
my mind about people not by what they look like
but by what's inside their hearts. Amen.*

Little Foxes

"Catch the foxes for us, the little foxes that are destroying our grape-fields, for the flowers are on the vines."
SONG OF SOLOMON 2:15

♥ ♥ ♥

Naughty little foxes nibble at the farmer's grapes, and before long the whole field is ruined. People can be like those little foxes. Sneaky sin says, "Come nibble on me," and people give in. They do what they know is wrong. When you are tempted to do something wrong, will you do the right thing, or will you be a naughty little fox?

Dear God, if sneaky sin tries to trick me, help me to do what is right. I don't want to be like those naughty little foxes. Amen.

Check Yourself Out

Let us test and look over our ways, and return to the Lord.
LAMENTATIONS 3:40

♥ ♥ ♥

Here are three little questions for you to answer. Do you pray every day? Are you doing your best to learn about Jesus? Do you always do what you know is right? The Bible says that you should check yourself out once in a while to see if you are living the way God wants. If you answered no to a question, that's okay! Everyone messes up sometimes. Just keep trying to do your best.

Dear God, I promise to do my best to pray every day,
learn about Jesus, and do what is right. Amen.

Hey, Look What I Did!

You might say to yourself, "I am rich because of my own power and strength," but remember the LORD your God!

DEUTERONOMY 8:17–18 NCV

♥ ♥ ♥

Name one thing you did that made you feel good about yourself. Maybe you won a race or received a reward. Maybe you did something really well and people said, "Wow, look what you did!" It's nice to feel pleased when you do a good job, but you should always remember to thank God. Without His help you couldn't do those things.

Thank You, God, for helping me to do things that make me feel good about myself. Amen.

Share the Leftovers

God can give you all you need. He will give you more than enough. You will have everything you need for yourselves. And you will have enough left over to give when there is a need.

2 CORINTHIANS 9:8

♥ ♥ ♥

Many times God blesses you with more than you need. When that happens, share the leftovers! If you have more than enough food, share what is left with those who are hungry. If you have good clothes that don't fit anymore, you can give them to kids who need them. Can you think of other ways to share what God gave you?

Dear God, will You show me, please, where I can share my leftovers? Amen.

Try, Try Again

The man who does not give up when tests come is happy.
After the test is over, he will receive the crown of life.
God has promised this to those who love Him.

JAMES 1:12

♥ ♥ ♥

If you try to do something but it doesn't work out, don't give up. Sometimes God tests His people. He wants them to become strong at being patient when working toward a goal. Keep working at those things you can't do yet. Keep trying. Before long, you will do all kinds of things that you thought you couldn't do!

Dear God, sometimes I feel like giving up.
Will You help me to keep on trying? Amen.

Yes, I Can!

"Stop doubting and believe."

JOHN 20:27 NIV

♥ ♥ ♥

Do you ever feel nervous about trying something new? Your heart goes *pitter-pat* really fast, and you say to yourself, *I don't think I can do this.* Many kids feel the same way you do. Growing up is about trying new things and learning. But there's nothing to be afraid of. God knows that you can do those new things! He knows because He will be right there with you. Remember—the next time you say, "I can't," God says you can!

Dear God, when I feel nervous about trying something new,
I will remember that You are right there with me. Amen.

If I Fall

But when he saw the strong wind, he was afraid. He began to go down in the water. He cried out, "Lord, save me!"
MATTHEW 14:30

♥ ♥ ♥

Maybe when you learned to swim, someone held you safe in the water so you wouldn't drown. Or maybe the first time you rode a two-wheeled bike you were afraid of falling and someone was there to catch you. God is always there to help when you feel afraid. All you have to do is say, "Lord, save me!" Then believe that He will.

Dear God, I know that whenever I feel afraid, I can count on You to help me. You will always—always—be at my side. Amen.

I Am God's Helper

Let no one show little respect for you because you are young.
Show other Christians how to live by your life. They should be
able to follow you in the way you talk and in what you do.

1 TIMOTHY 4:12

♥ ♥ ♥

You can be God's helper here on earth by talking and acting in ways that make Him proud of you. When you behave with good manners, other people will see. Your good manners will help God teach others the way He wants them to live. They will see your good manners and say, "I want to be like that child."

Dear God, I want to be Your helper. Please remind
me to have good manners all the time. Amen.

My Safe Place

The Lord also keeps safe those who suffer.
He is a safe place in times of trouble.

PSALM 9:9

♥ ♥ ♥

Imagine that you found a lost kitten on a rainy day. The kitten was wet and afraid. What would you do? You would probably rescue the kitten and take it someplace safe. What if you were lost and afraid? You could count on God for help. He is your safe place when you are in trouble. All you have to do is remember that He is with you. God loves you, and He will protect you.

Dear God, thank You for being my safest place. Amen.

I Am a Letter from Jesus!

*You are as a letter from Christ written
by us. You are not written as other letters
are written with ink, or on pieces of stone.
You are written in human hearts by
the Spirit of the living God.*

2 CORINTHIANS 3:3

♥ ♥ ♥

Think about this: you are like a letter—or a
text message—from Jesus to others. Whenever
you share with someone that Jesus loves him
or her, it's like a love letter from Jesus to that
person. You don't have to write it down. Just
tell others that Jesus loves them.

*Dear Jesus, I love You, and I will remember to
tell others that You love them, too. Amen.*

More Than Anything

Do not love the world or anything in the world.
If anyone loves the world, the Father's love is not in him.

1 JOHN 2:15

♥ ♥ ♥

Whom do you love best of all? Did you say, "God"? He wants you to put Him first and love Him most. It's good to love your family, friends, pets, and others. It's fine to say that you love soccer or school or yummy food like pizza. But no love should be greater than the love you have for God. The more you love Him, the more you will feel God's love filling up your heart.

Dear God, I love You more than anything. Amen.

Oh, No! It's a Pterosaur!

I will show you and teach you in the way you should go.
I will tell you what to do with My eye upon you.

PSALM 32:8

♥ ♥ ♥

Imagine that a pterosaur—a flying dinosaur—picked you up and plopped you down in the middle of nowhere. That's make-believe, of course, but imagine it. What would you do if you were lost in the middle of nowhere? Did you say, "I would ask God for help?" Whenever you feel like you don't know what to do, God promises to help you. He watches everything you do.

Dear God, I know You will always help me,
even when I feel like I'm lost. Amen.

Inside and Out

For You made the parts inside me.
You put me together inside my mother.
PSALM 139:13

♥ ♥ ♥

Look at yourself in a mirror. Your outside parts—skin, eyes, hair—are easy to see. But what about all your inside parts? You have a brain for thinking. Your lungs are for breathing. The heart is like a pump that moves blood through your body and keeps you alive. You have all kinds of inside parts that keep your body working. When God made your body, He thought of everything.

Dear God, thank You for every part of
my body, inside and out. Amen.

On Eagle's Wings

But they who wait upon the Lord will get new strength. They will rise up with wings like eagles. They will run and not get tired. They will walk and not become weak.

ISAIAH 40:31

♥ ♥ ♥

Imagine that you are lost in the middle of nowhere, and after a while God sends a big eagle to rescue you. The strong, friendly bird swoops down, lifts you safely onto its wings, and carries you home. Think of this make-believe story when you need God's help. He won't send a big bird to lift you up, but be patient. He will find a way to rescue you.

Dear God, I feel safe knowing that You will protect me. Amen.

"I Want That!"

*I am not saying I need anything. I have
learned to be happy with whatever I have.*

PHILIPPIANS 4:11

♥ ♥ ♥

Imagine that you are in a store with your mom or dad and you see something you want. "I want that!" you say. But your parent says, "You can't have it." How would you feel?

You can't have everything you want, but God gives you exactly what you need. Thank Him for what He has given you. Learn to be happy with what you have.

*Dear God, thank You for meeting all my needs.
Help me to be happy with what I have. Amen.*

"I'm So Proud of You!"

*Do as God would do. Much-loved
children want to do as their fathers do.*

EPHESIANS 5:1

♥ ♥ ♥

Your parents are proud of you because you are their child and they love you. But they're extra proud when you behave well and obey their rules. Your heavenly Father loves you, too—more than anyone! And He's extra proud of you when you follow His rules and live the way He wants you to. What could you do today to make your heavenly Father extra proud?

*Dear God, You love me so much, and I want
everything I do to make You proud of me. Amen.*

Laugh and Sing a Song

Then we were filled with laughter, and we sang
happy songs. Then the other nations said,
"The LORD has done great things for them."

PSALM 126:2 NCV

♥ ♥ ♥

The sounds of children playing are like music to God's ears. He loves hearing His children laugh and sing happy songs. Whenever you feel so happy that you want to laugh and sing, remember that it's because God has done something good for you. Name one good thing He has done for you today.

Dear God, because You are so good to us all, I want
the whole world to laugh, sing, and be happy. Amen.

Cheerful Little Words

Worry is a heavy load, but a kind word cheers you up.

PROVERBS 12:25 NCV

♥ ♥ ♥

Close your eyes and think of three kind things you could say to cheer someone up. Maybe you said, "I love you," or "It will get better," or "Smile because God thinks you are wonderful." There are many kind things you can say to help people feel better. Maybe you know someone who could use some cheering up today. Say a little prayer and ask God to help you find just the right words.

Dear God, I know somebody who needs cheering up.
I need You to help me with the best words to say. Amen.

Smile. . .Smile. . .Smile

As a face is reflected in water,
so the heart reflects the real person.
PROVERBS 27:19 NLT

♥ ♥ ♥

Look at your face in a mirror. Is it a happy face?
A grumpy face? A sad face? A silly face? An
angry face? Maybe it's just an everyday face
with no special feeling. The Bible teaches that
your face shows others what is in your heart.
God wants you to have a smiling face because
smiles are contagious. If you smile at someone,
maybe that person will smile back. Give it a try!

Dear God, I have the very best reason to smile:
it's because You live in my heart! Amen.

Jesus, King of Kings

The Lord is King forever and ever.
PSALM 10:16

♥ ♥ ♥

Many stories are written about kings. Some are make-believe stories with kings that do mean things or silly things or brave things. Others are true stories about real-life kings who live now or lived long ago.

Have you met a king? Yes, you have! You know Jesus, and the Bible says that He is the King of all kings. Jesus has ruled heaven and earth from the beginning of time, and He will rule forever. Aren't you glad that you are one of God's kids?

Dear Jesus, I'm happy to be in Your kingdom, and I think it's awesome that You know me and love me. Amen.

What Is Love?

Love is not rude, is not selfish, and does not get upset with others. Love does not count up wrongs that have been done.

1 Corinthians 13:5 NCV

♥ ♥ ♥

The Bible tells us what love is. Love is being patient, kind, and never jealous. Love is not bragging or thinking you are better than someone. Love is when you are polite and unselfish. Love is when you don't get upset with others or keep track of the wrong things they do. Love is being honest, doing what is right, trusting, and hoping. That's love!

Dear God, I didn't know there were so many different ways to love. Thank You for teaching me. Amen.

Trustworthy

"You have been faithful over a few things.
I will put many things in your care."

MATTHEW 25:21

♥ ♥ ♥

Trustworthy is a big word that means people can depend on you. When you do a great job with simple things, your parents and teachers will trust you with more important things. It's the same with God. When you obey Him and show that He can trust you, then He will lead you to do great things for Him. Do your very best at everything you do. Show the whole world that you are trustworthy!

Dear God, help me to be someone
whom everyone can trust. Amen.

God's Treasure Chest

Let my instructions be your greatest treasure.

PROVERBS 7:2 CEV

♥ ♥ ♥

Where do you keep your treasures? Maybe you have a little box for your special things. Maybe you take them with you in a backpack. Your treasures are important to you, and you don't want to lose them or allow them to get broken. God wants your greatest treasure to be the Bible. The treasure chest can be your heart. Remember your Bible verses and keep them inside your heart. Then you will always be able to find them.

Dear God, Your words are my most important treasure,
and I will keep them inside my heart. Amen.

Working for the Lord

Whatever work you do, do it with all your heart.
Do it for the Lord and not for men.

COLOSSIANS 3:23

♥ ♥ ♥

"This is too hard! I give up." Everyone feels that way sometimes. Life is all about working and learning new things. The Bible says that whatever you do, you should do it with your whole heart and remember that you are doing it for Jesus! When He gives you something to do, it will never be too hard. You can always trust Him to help you.

Dear God, when something is hard, I won't give up.
I will trust You to help me get it done. Amen.

Pray about Everything

Do not worry. Learn to pray about everything.
Give thanks to God as you ask Him for what you need.

PHILIPPIANS 4:6

♥ ♥ ♥

When you pray, you tell God what you need, and you thank Him for what you have. But do you tell Him what you worry about? Do you tell Him if you have been naughty? You should never feel afraid or embarrassed to tell God everything. He sees all you do, so nothing will surprise Him. God always listens to your prayers. He loves you. He wants you to tell Him everything.

Dear God, thank You that I can feel comfortable
talking to You about everything. Amen.

Plug Into God's Power

Finally, be strong in the Lord and in his mighty power.
EPHESIANS 6:10 NIV

♥ ♥ ♥

Phones, laptops, and tablets; they all need to be plugged in to recharge. If they don't get plugged in, what happens? It's like they're dead inside. Think about this: God is a power source for people! You can't connect with Him unless you plug into Him by praying and learning what's in the Bible. God's power is mighty. It will keep you going for the rest of your life.

Dear God, I promise to plug into Your power every day by praying and learning more about You. Amen.

God's Angels

Therefore, angels are only servants—spirits sent
to care for people who will inherit salvation.
HEBREWS 1:14 NLT

♥ ♥ ♥

Angels are God's heavenly helpers. They work for Him, and their job is to care for God's people here on earth. All day, all night, God sends His angels on special assignments. Angels are with you wherever you go: at home, on the playground, in school, everywhere! When you go to sleep at night, God's angels watch over you. You can't see them, but they are there. God has countless angels, more than enough to watch over everyone on earth.

Dear God, thank You for angels that watch over me. Amen.

I Saw an Angel!

*Remember to welcome strangers, because some who
have done this have welcomed angels without knowing it.*
HEBREWS 13:2 NCV

♥ ♥ ♥

It's important always to have a parent or another trusted adult with you when you meet a stranger. Can you think of a time when a stranger did something kind for you? That person may have given you a little gift or helped you in a special way. The Bible says that a stranger might be one of God's angels sent to do something just for you. So keep your eyes open. Maybe someday you will see an angel!

*Dear God, please open up my eyes to see
Your angels here on earth. Amen.*

Tricky Traps

My eyes are always on the LORD, for he rescues me from the traps of my enemies.
PSALM 25:15 NLT

♥ ♥ ♥

"Ha-ha! I tricked you!" Sometimes silly tricks are fun to play on others. Other times tricks are not fun, especially if someone tries to trap you into doing something you know is wrong. Jesus says that if you keep your eyes on Him, He will rescue you from those tricky traps. Think about Jesus all day long. Trust Him to show you right from wrong.

Dear Jesus, I trust You to rescue me from any tricky traps. Thank You for helping me. Amen.

Jesus Says, "I'm Here!"

At once Jesus talked to them. He said,
"Take hope. It is I, do not be afraid."

MARK 6:50

♥ ♥ ♥

When Jesus' followers felt afraid, Jesus told them He was there and not to be afraid. They never had to fear anything because Jesus was always with them. Jesus is with you, too, every day, all the time. Whenever something is scary, all you have to do is remember that Jesus is bigger and stronger than everything. Jesus will take care of you.

Dear Jesus, if I am worried or afraid, I will remember
Your words and trust You to protect me. Amen.

I've Got Jesus Power!

"LORD, only you can help weak people against the strong.
Help us, LORD our God, because we depend on you."

2 CHRONICLES 14:11 NCV

♥ ♥ ♥

You might be little, but you have an amazing superpower—it's Jesus Power! You get it by trusting Jesus to help you stand up to whatever gets in your way. If you feel weak, Jesus will make you strong. He is the only one who can. All you have to do is whisper a prayer, and He will fill you up with power. Ask Him to do it right now.

Dear Jesus, please fill me up, right now,
with Your super Jesus Power! Amen.

Talent Show

*God has given each of you a gift from his great variety
of spiritual gifts. Use them well to serve one another.*

1 PETER 4:10 NLT

♥ ♥ ♥

Do you and your friends play talent show? A talent show is an
activity where people sing and dance and share with one another
the special things they can do. God gives everyone things they are
good at. Can you name three things you are good at? Don't be shy
about sharing your talent with others. God gave you that special
gift, and He wants you to share it with everyone.

Dear God, thank You for giving me things I am good at. Amen.

Alone with God

*But when you pray, go away by yourself, shut the
door behind you, and pray to your Father in private.
Then your Father, who sees everything, will reward you.*
MATTHEW 6:6 NLT

♥ ♥ ♥

People pray together at home and at church. But sometimes God
wants alone time with His children. Jesus said that everyone should
go to their room, shut the door, and pray to God. It's a special time
with God when you can tell Him everything that is on your mind.
Do you spend time alone with God every day?

*Dear God, I like spending time with You alone.
Thank You for hearing my prayers. Amen.*

Good-Bye Stony, Stubborn Heart!

*I will take away their stony, stubborn heart
and give them a tender, responsive heart.*
EZEKIEL 11:19 NLT

♥ ♥ ♥

Think about an old, dried-up sponge. It feels hard as stone, and
it's not good for anything. But if you pour water into that sponge,
it becomes soft and squishy again. You can use it as if it's brand-
new. Some people have hearts that act like dried-up sponges. But
if you pour Jesus' love into those hearts, they will be like new—soft
and loving. Is your heart hard, or is it filled up with Jesus?

*Dear Jesus, please give me a soft, gentle heart.
Fill it up with Your love. Amen.*

My Family

*My people will live in safety, quietly
at home. They will be at rest.*
ISAIAH 32:18 NLT

♥ ♥ ♥

God loves families. He puts them together
just right—mothers, fathers, brothers, sisters,
and others. No two families are alike. Each is
special in its own way. When everyone in a
family knows Jesus, all family members feel
more comfortable and safer at home. Does
everyone in your family know Him? You can
help your family know Jesus by sharing what
you have learned about Him.

*Dear Jesus, I want everyone in my
family to know You. Help me to
teach them to love You. Amen.*

GoD's Big, Happy Family

God decided in advance to adopt us into his own family
by bringing us to himself through Jesus Christ. This is
what he wanted to do, and it gave him great pleasure.
EPHESIANS 1:5 NLT

♥ ♥ ♥

Can you name everyone in your family? Maybe you forgot one—God! Everyone who knows Jesus is a member of God's family. The Bible says that God adopts them as His own. Whenever someone asks Jesus into his or her heart, that person becomes a member of God's family—and that makes God very happy.

Dear God, thank You for reminding me that I am
a member of two families, mine and Yours! Amen.

Love One Another

Christ accepted you, so you should accept
each other, which will bring glory to God.
ROMANS 15:7 NCV

♥ ♥ ♥

Think about it. Everyone is different. God made us to look different. He gave us different things that we are good at. He has a special plan for each of our lives. God loves all of us just the way we are, and that's how He wants us to love one another. What someone looks like or does shouldn't matter. God made us all, and He is honored when we love one another.

Dear God, I want to love everyone like You do.
Will You help me, please? Amen.

Be a Deer

The Lord God is my strength. He has made my feet like the feet of a deer, and He makes me walk on high places.
HABAKKUK 3:19

♥ ♥ ♥

The Bible sometimes uses animals to teach about God. Habakkuk 3:19 uses deer to remind you to be sure of yourself with God's help. Deer can run very fast, but they always know where they are going. They climb high hills carefully without being afraid of falling. God wants you to be like those deer. Trust that He will help you to make good choices and know where you are going.

Dear God, when I trust You to lead me, You help me feel safe and strong. Thank You, God. Amen.

Wait a Minute!

Wait for the Lord. Be strong. Let your
heart be strong. Yes, wait for the Lord.
PSALM 27:14

♥ ♥ ♥

You are ready to go someplace fun, and your mom says, "Wait a minute." How do you act when you have to wait? Do you say, "Hurry up. Let's go!"? God allows us to wait for an important reason—to teach us patience. Patience is good to learn because it reminds us that God is in control. The next time someone tells you, "Wait a minute," think of it as God's little test. Show Him how patient you can be.

Dear God, I will do my best always to be patient. Amen.

Know-It-All!

Don't depend on your own wisdom.
Respect the LORD and refuse to do wrong.
PROVERBS 3:7 NCV

♥ ♥ ♥

Who is the smartest person you know? Do you think that person knows everything? Some people are smart, but the only one who knows everything is God. He knows what is happening right now and what will happen in the future. He sees everything everyone does all the time. No one can know what God knows. That is one reason why God is so powerful. He is our great Know-It-All God.

Dear God, I'm thankful that when I have questions,
You have all the answers. Amen.

God's Love Is So Big

But why are people even important to you?
Why do you take care of human beings?

PSALM 8:4 NCV

♥ ♥ ♥

King David looked at the night sky and thought about God. He saw the moon and stars. He knew that no one on earth could ever make something so big. David realized how small he was compared to God's sky, and he wondered, *Why does God even care about people?* Do you know the answer? God cares about people because He made us! His love for us is bigger than all His creations.

Dear God, I might be small, but You love
me so big! I love You, too. Amen.

Too Much Stuff!

"You will have such a surplus of crops that you will need to
clear out the old grain to make room for the new harvest!"

LEVITICUS 26:10 NLT

♥ ♥ ♥

God often blesses people with more than they need. Then they have to clear out the old to make room for the new. What can you do with your old stuff? You can give it to someone who needs it. You can give away clothes you have outgrown and toys you no longer play with. When you have too much of anything, you can share it with others!

Dear God, when I have more than I need,
please remind me to share. Amen.

Get Busy!

People harvest only what they plant.
GALATIANS 6:7 NCV

♥ ♥ ♥

What would happen if a farmer wanted a field of corn but he never planted the seeds? No corn! It takes work to get what you want. Do you want to draw a picture? You have to get out your paper and crayons. Do you want to play a new game? You have to learn the rules. If you want to learn the piano, you have to practice. Think about it: if you do nothing, then nothing will ever get done. So get busy and do some work today.

*Dear God, I promise to get busy
and get things done. Amen.*

God's Not Done Yet

God began doing a good work in you, and I am sure he will continue it until it is finished when Jesus Christ comes again.
PHILLIPIANS 1:6 NCV

♥ ♥ ♥

Some great artists work on one piece of art for months, even years, before everything is done just right. God is the greatest artist of all. And YOU are His creation! He began working on you before you were born. He will keep working on you every day of your life. When you get to heaven someday, God will look at you and say, "I did a great job. Now you are perfect!"

Dear God, thank You for making me a work of art! Amen.

Boo-Hoo!

You keep track of all my sorrows. You have collected all my tears in your bottle. You have recorded each one in your book.
PSALM 56:8 NLT

♥ ♥ ♥

When was the last time you cried? God cares so much for you that He knows each time you cry. He writes it in His book, and He collects all your tears in a bottle. God wants His children to be happy. The next time you feel like crying, see if you can put on a happy face instead. If you can't, that's okay, too—God understands.

Dear God, whenever I cry, I will remember that You want me to be happy. Amen.

God Will Make It Better

*"For I will change their sorrow to joy, and will
comfort them. I will give them joy for their sorrow."*
JEREMIAH 31:13

♥ ♥ ♥

What makes it better when you feel sad? Maybe a hug. Maybe someone's kind, gentle words. Do you know that God promises to change your sadness to joy? When you feel unhappy, you can talk to God about it. Ask Him to share His joyfulness with you. Sing Him a song. Tell Him a funny story. God is right there with you, ready to help you feel happy again.

*Dear God, whenever I am sad, I can count
on You to help make it better. Amen.*

Let's Play!

And the city will be filled with boys and girls playing.
ZECHARIAH 8:5

♥ ♥ ♥

God fills up the world with child-friendly places and fun things for children to do. He also gives childrens friends, brothers and sisters, and other family members to play with. When you and your friends play, what do you like to do? Maybe you go to the playground or play dress-up or enjoy games. God wants His children to have fun. So play. But play safely. And remember to thank God for all the fun things He gives you to do.

Thank You, God, for play, and for friends to play with. Amen.

Thank God!

I will honor the Lord at all times.
His praise will always be in my mouth.

PSALM 34:1

♥ ♥ ♥

God is so great! He deserves a big thank-you for the many wonderful things He does. Can you name some of them right now? You could thank God for creating you, for your family, for friends and your pets, and on and on! If you think about it, you will never run out of things to thank God for. When you say your prayers, don't forget to say, "Thank You, God!" He loves to hear those words.

Thank You, God, for everything! I love You so much. Amen.

Forget aBout It!

"I will show loving-kindness to them and forgive
their sins. I will remember their sins no more."

HEBREWS 8:12

Maybe your sister, brother, or friend does things sometimes that make you angry or hurt your feelings. Do you remember those things? Could you count how many times they've happened? God says, "Forget about it!" He wants you to be more like Him. God keeps on loving people when we make Him angry. He forgives us and forgets what we have done. Can you do that, too?

Dear God, please help me to be loving
and forgiving like You are. Amen.

God's Armor

Therefore put on the full armor of God, so that when
the day of evil comes, you may be able to stand your
ground, and after you have done everything, to stand.
EPHESIANS 6:13 NIV

♥ ♥ ♥

Knights wore suits of armor to protect themselves from enemies' weapons. Did you know that God gave you a special kind of armor? You can't see it, but it's there inside your heart. It's things like telling the truth, obeying God, studying the Bible, and having faith that God will protect you. When you put on God's armor, nothing can hurt you.

Dear God, when I feel afraid, remind me that
I'm wearing Your special suit of armor. Amen.

Be a Good Example

These things show us something. They teach us not to
want things that are bad for us like those people did.

1 CORINTHIANS 10:6

♥ ♥ ♥

Are you a people watcher? People watchers notice how others around them behave. Some people behave well. You can tell by their words and actions that they are kind and respectful. Other people might be rude and disrespectful. What do you think people watchers notice when they see you? God wants you to set a good example by being on your best behavior all the time.

Dear God, I will do my very best to show
others my best behavior all the time. Amen.

Good Night, Sleep Tight

I will lie down and sleep in peace.
O Lord, You alone keep me safe.

PSALM 4:8

♥ ♥ ♥

Bedtime is that special time when you fold your hands and say your prayers. Then, snuggled safe and warm in bed, it's time for a little sleep, a little rest. God is with you all through the night. He never sleeps. He stays at your bedside watching over you.

Just before you fall asleep tonight, say this little poem:

Good night. Sleep tight.
God is here with me tonight.

Dear God, my sleep tonight will be oh,
so sweet because You watch over me. Amen.

Precious

*I will always love you; that's why I've been
so patient and kind. You are precious to me.*
JEREMIAH 31:3–4 CEV

♥ ♥ ♥

Precious is a word that describes something so
expensive that most people can't afford to buy
it. Some precious things can't be bought with
all the money in the world. That is the kind of
precious you are to God. You are so important
and loved by Him that He will never let you
go. Nothing is worth more to God than you!

*Dear God, I feel so loved by You,
and do You know what? I think
You are precious, too! Amen.*

Listen to God's Words

But don't just listen to God's word.
You must do what it says. Otherwise,
you are only fooling yourselves.
JAMES 1:22 NLT

♥ ♥ ♥

The Bible is God's Book. Long ago He told some men to write down His words. The Bible is one way that God speaks to you. When someone reads to you from the Bible, listen hard to the words. God wants you not just to hear them but also to learn from them and do what He says. Can you name something you have learned from the Bible?

Dear God, please help me to remember
that You speak to me through the
words in the Bible. Amen.

God Is Love

Those who do not love do not know God because God is love.

1 JOHN 4:8

♥ ♥ ♥

What do you love to do? God made those things for you to enjoy. Name the people who love you. God created them and gave them to you. Now think about what makes you feel loved. God made hugs, cuddles, and kindness just for you. God loves you so much that He fills your life with love. So whenever you love something or feel loved, remember that God is love. Everything He does is because He loves you.

> *Dear God, fill me up every day with Your great love.*
> *Give me plenty so I can share it with everyone. Amen.*

The World's Only Superhero

"In the world you will have much trouble.
But take hope! I have power over the world!"

JOHN 16:33

♥ ♥ ♥

Who is the world's superhero? Did you say, "Jesus"? Jesus has power over the whole world. He told His followers that the world will always have trouble. But Jesus also promised them that He is much more powerful than any bad thing that can ever happen. Jesus is the world's only superhero! That's why when trouble gets in your way, you can always count on Him for help.

> *Dear Jesus, whatever happens in the world,*
> *I know that You will keep me safe. Amen.*

GoD's Love Is Forever

Even when you are old I will be the same. And even when
your hair turns white, I will help you. I will take care of
what I have made. I will carry you, and will save you.

ISAIAH 46:4

♥ ♥ ♥

How old are you? Who is the oldest person you know? God loves
old people, young people, and all people just the same. God's love
never changes. No matter how old you are, God will take care of
you. He will help you and protect you for as long as you live—even
when you are very old and your hair turns white!

Dear God, I'm glad Your love is forever. Amen.

GoD Protects His People

*Our enemies were trying to frighten us and to keep us
from our work. But I asked God to give me strength.*
NEHEMIAH 6:9 CEV

♥ ♥ ♥

After Jesus went back to heaven, His friends worked to tell the whole world about the wonderful things Jesus had done. But some people didn't like Jesus. They didn't want the world to know about Him. They did mean things and tried to stop Jesus' friends. But they couldn't! God protected His friends. They went on telling about Jesus, and that's why today the whole world knows about Him.

*Dear Jesus, I am Your friend, and I am
not afraid to tell others about You. Amen.*

Follow the Rules

*Anyone who runs in a race must
follow the rules to get the crown.*
2 TIMOTHY 2:5

♥ ♥ ♥

You are running a race with kids from your school. You are ahead and racing toward the finish line. Then a child bumps into you on purpose. He pushes you! Down you go, in a lump, while he wins the race. He came in first, but he didn't get the prize because he didn't follow the rules. God wants everyone to follow rules. Whether you win or lose, it's more important that you always play fair.

*Dear God, in whatever I do, I promise to
play fair and follow the rules. Amen.*

GOD IS ON MY SIDE

*If God is on our side,
can anyone be against us?*
ROMANS 8:31 CEV

♥ ♥ ♥

When you are trying hard to learn something new, God is your best cheerleader. Think of Him saying to you, "You can do it! I know you can." If someone ever makes you feel like you are not good enough or smart enough, tell God about it. He knows you are the best of His creations. If someone doesn't like you, it doesn't matter because God loves you all the time. He is your best friend, and He will always be on your side.

*Thank You, God, for being
my very best friend. Amen.*

GOD Can Do It!

Jesus said, "God can do things men cannot do."
LUKE 18:27

♥ ♥ ♥

There are some things that only God can do. People can't make the sun shine or the rain stop falling. They can't make fluffy white clouds into shapes that look like a horse or a duck or a hippo. People can't make the sky blue or create a shooting star. Only God can do those things. Can you think of other things that only God can do? When you say to yourself, *That's impossible*, remember that God can do anything.

*Dear God, whenever I think that can't be done,
I will remember—God can do it. Amen.*

Fishing for Men

Jesus said to them, "Follow Me.
I will make you fish for men!"
MATTHEW 4:19

♥ ♥ ♥

Jesus saw men fishing. "Follow Me," Jesus said. "I will make you fish for men." Jesus meant that He wanted the fishermen to get people to believe that Jesus had come to save them from sin. He wanted the fishermen to become great teachers who would tell the whole world about Jesus. That's what the fishermen did. Instead of bringing in buckets of fish, they brought in big crowds of people who learned to believe in Jesus and follow Him.

Dear God, I promise to tell people about You,
just like the fishermen did. Amen.

GOD'S BIG TENT

During danger he will keep me safe in his shelter. He will hide me in his Holy Tent, or he will keep me safe on a high mountain.
PSALM 27:5 NCV

♥ ♥ ♥

Have you ever slept outside in a tent? A tent helps you feel safe. It protects you from rain, bugs, and anything else that might disturb your sleep. When you go to bed tonight, imagine that God's love is like a tent. It covers you and helps you to feel safe all night long.

Sweet dreams. Sleep tight.
God will keep you safe tonight!

Dear God, thank You for covering me with Your love. Amen.

Quiet Prayers

Then He went away by Himself to pray in a desert.
LUKE 5:16

♥ ♥ ♥

Jesus liked being with people. Big crowds followed Him wherever He went. But sometimes Jesus needed to go off by Himself to have a quiet talk with His Father, God. Do you sometimes feel like you need to be alone and quiet? You can pray to God wherever you are, even in the noisiest places. But it's good to have quiet prayers when you can relax, feel close to God, and tell Him what's on your mind.

Dear God, let's spend some quiet time together so I can tell you about my day. Amen.

Big Prayers, Little Prayers

I am praying to you because I know you will answer,
O God. Bend down and listen as I pray.
PSALM 17:6 NLT

♥ ♥ ♥

You can talk with God all day by saying little prayers like, "I love You, God," or "Thank You for helping me, God," or "I really like that beautiful butterfly You made, God!" He loves hearing your little prayers. And He loves big prayers when you talk with Him for a long time and tell Him what's on your mind. Whether your prayers are big or little, God hears them because He loves you.

Thank You, God, for hearing my prayers. Amen.

God's Children

The lives of all people belong to me—
parents as well as children.
EZEKIEL 18:4 CEV

♥ ♥ ♥

Does God have kids? Yes, He does. Jesus is God's Son. You are
one of God's kids, too! And so are your parents. All the people on
earth who have ever lived or are alive right now or will live in the
future belong to God. He created every one to be His own child. It
doesn't matter to God whether a person is a newborn baby or one
hundred years old. God is their heavenly Father—forever.

Dear heavenly Father, I'm glad that I'm Your child. Amen.

A Parent's Job

Bring up a child by teaching him the way he should go,
and when he is old he will not turn away from it.
PROVERBS 22:6

♥ ♥ ♥

A parent's most important job is to teach their kids to love God
and do what He says. When kids learn to love God and follow His
ways, they will grow up to be adults who love God and follow Him.
Talk with your mom or dad about God. Ask questions and read
the Bible together. Obey your parents, and remember that they
are God's helpers.

Dear God, thank You for my parents.
I will try to obey them all the time. Amen.

A KID'S JOB

The father of one who is right with
God will have much joy. He who has
a wise son will be glad in him.
PROVERBS 23:24

♥ ♥ ♥

A kid's most important job is to learn to love God and do what He says. God is very wise, and when you follow His ways, then you become wise, too. When you live to please God, you will make God and your parents happy. Someday you might be a parent. Then you can teach your own children to love God and learn to follow His ways.

Dear God, please give me wisdom to
live in a way that pleases You. Amen.

GOD HOLDS MY HAND

*"For I am the Lord your God Who holds your right hand,
and Who says to you, 'Do not be afraid. I will help you.' "*

ISAIAH 41:13

♥ ♥ ♥

When you cross the street or walk in a crowd, a grown-up helps you stay safe by holding your hand. Do you know that God holds your hand, too? Hold up your right hand. God holds that hand. He says, "Don't be afraid. I will help you." You can't feel God holding your hand, but He does. How do you know? Because the Bible says so!

*Dear God, whenever I feel afraid, I will remember
that You are holding my hand. Amen.*

Ah–Ah–Choo!

The Lord will give him strength on his bed of sickness.
When he is sick, You will make him well again.

PSALM 41:3

♥ ♥ ♥

A runny nose. A big, wet sneeze. A rumble-tumble upset tummy.
Being sick is no fun! That sick, icky feeling keeps you from doing
all the fun things you enjoy. Jesus understands how sick people
feel. When He lived on earth, He helped the sick get well again.
Jesus will help you, too. The next time you don't feel good, ask
Jesus to help you. Then trust that He will.

Dear Jesus, when I feel sick, I will trust
You to help me feel better again. Amen.

Get Some Rest

He said to them, "Come away from the people.
Be by yourselves and rest."

MARK 6:31

♥ ♥ ♥

Have you been to a crowded, loud place and said to yourself, *I just want to go home?* Sometimes it feels good to get away from people and noise. Jesus felt that way, too. He understood that everyone needs quiet time alone to rest. Some people rest by taking a nap. Others enjoy a short rest while relaxing outside and looking up at the clouds. What is your favorite way to rest?

Thank You, Jesus, for peaceful times when
I can calm down, rest, and relax. Amen.

Sadness to Gladness

Blessed are they that mourn: for they shall be comforted.
MATTHEW 5:4 KJV

♥ ♥ ♥

Jesus stood on top of a hill so He could speak to a huge crowd of people. He taught them about God. Jesus said, "People who are sad can be happy because God will comfort them." God is the best comforter of all. He knows when you are sad, and He wants to change your sadness to gladness. That's why Jesus said, "Be happy!" God will find a way to comfort you whenever you feel sad.

Dear God, it makes me feel good knowing that You can change my sadness to gladness. Amen.

Live Like Jesus

Put out of your life all these things: bad feelings about other people, anger, temper, loud talk, bad talk which hurts other people, and bad feelings which hurt other people.

EPHESIANS 4:31

♥ ♥ ♥

If you want to keep Satan away, do your best to live like Jesus. Only have good feelings about other people. Watch your temper. Don't use language that is disrespectful or hurts others. Jesus was gentle and kind. He loved everyone and was helpful. Can you think of other ways that you can be more like Him?

Dear Jesus, help me to learn more about You so I can be more like You. Amen.

Hooray for You!

Therefore encourage one another and build
each other up, just as in fact you are doing.
1 THESSALONIANS 5:11 NIV

♥ ♥ ♥

Imagine that you are playing baseball and running for home base.
From the stands you hear your family cheering you on. "You can
do it!" "Good job!" "Keep going; we love you!" It feels good to hear
them encouraging you, doesn't it? God wants everyone to be an
encourager. Can you think of three things to say when you see
someone trying hard?

Dear God, I want to be an encourager. When I see people trying
hard to do something, please remind me to cheer them on. Amen.

I'll Help You Feel Better

*He gives us comfort in all our troubles. Then we can
comfort other people who have the same troubles.
We give the same kind of comfort God gives us.*

2 CORINTHIANS 1:4

♥ ♥ ♥

God understands sadness. When you feel sad, He knows that your parents' hugs and cuddles will make you feel better. He knows that kind, gentle words will help. God knows exactly what to do to chase away your sadness. When someone you know feels sad, remember what helped you feel better. Then you can use what you learned to help others.

*Dear God, when someone I know is unhappy,
please help me know how to make them feel better. Amen.*

Helping Others

Let us help each other to love others and to do good.
HEBREWS 10:24

♥ ♥ ♥

Jesus wants us to help one another be loving and caring. Maybe you know someone who is grumpy and unkind. You can teach that person to love others by setting a good example. When you are kind and do good things for others, you show them God's love. It doesn't matter if they are kind in return. What's important is that they see you acting as Jesus would—showing lovingkindness to everyone you meet.

Dear God, please help me to be kind to others,
even when they are grumpy. Amen.

Let's Plant Some God Seeds!

"This is what the picture-story means.
The seed is the Word of God."

LUKE 8:11

♥ ♥ ♥

Jesus told a story about seeds that grew into big, strong plants. He said the seeds were like the Word of God. The Word of God is the Bible. The Bible is made up of many small parts called verses. Each chapter in this book begins with a Bible verse. Learning Bible verses is like planting God's seeds in your heart. The Bible helps you to grow strong in your love for God and to obey Him in all that you do.

Dear God, as I learn the Bible, please make
Your words grow in my heart. Amen.

About the Author

Jean Fischer has been writing for children for nearly three decades and has served as an editor with Golden Books. She has written with Thomas Kinkade, John MacArthur, and Adventures in Odyssey, and she's one of the authors for Barbour's Camp Club Girls series. A nature lover, Jean lives in Racine, Wisconsin.

Now I Lay Me Down to Sleep

Bedtime Prayers & Promises for Little Hearts

This entry in Barbour's popular Bedtime Bible series for kids 5 to 8 is a fantastic reminder that God keeps His promises while also encouraging young hearts to spend time talking to God each day. *Bedtime Prayers and Promises for Little Hearts* encourages parents and kids to spend quality faith-building time together.

Paperback / 978-1-63058-899-1 / $7.99

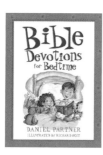

Bible Devotions for Bedtime

Going a step beyond Bible stories, this fun devotional book challenges children ages 5 to 8 to stop and think about the meaning of each account. More than five dozen devotions are drawn from the breadth of scripture—from the Creation to Revelation—and are brightly illustrated, in full color, for young readers' pleasure. *Bible Devotions for Bedtime* is perfect for parents wanting to spend spiritual "quality time" with their kids!

Paperback / 978-1-59310-358-3 / $5.99